Goal:
101 Ways Two School Teachers Became Millionaires By The Age Of 43
(No Excuses! I Have Had 9 Brain Surgeries So Don't Feel Sorry For Yourself. Set Your Goals In Life And Achieve Them!)
By: Scott Schell

I always get frustrated when people say they can't get ahead or they will never be able to do something. I say to those people- get focused and you need to set some big life driving goals. From an early age, I set some major goals. In life, we all have struggles. The bigger the struggle the more reason/drive you have to achieve your goal. When I was in 6th grade, I was diagnosed with Hydrocephalus and had to have 6 brain surgeries (1 surgery was an emergency surgery because my vitals crashed and I almost died).   Before the surgeries, I was struggling in school and I lost my coordination to play sports. After the surgeries, I could no longer play contact sports. I had to work extra hard at school because it took longer to memorize things. It even took me 3 times to remember my best friend's name- Scott, same name as mine. I tell you all this to say, "Who cares." I don't have it that bad and if I want something, I should set a goal and don't stop until I achieve it. After being in the hospital, I don't feel sorry about anybody's situation (ask my wife- I don't give sympathy out). In the hospital, I saw kids with terminally ill diseases. Those are the people my heart goes out to. I was in the hospital for only a week at a time, but some kids have long stays in the hospital. When I left the hospital, I was able to resume my goals in life. I tell you this because life is short. You could tell yourself, I'll travel when I retire or I'm going to … in the future. You may have several goals that you want to achieve when you or 65 to 70. I never set goals for the end of my life; I want to set goals that I can achieve in 15-20 years at most. If you don't have a plan, then you aren't really taking any steps that will help you achieve your goal. You will always feel sorry for yourself and your situation. Also, who knows if you're going to be around in 50 years (all you 20 year olds out there). Time is precious and you better try to meet your goals A.S.A.P. You have to come up with a goal and get focused on that goal. Time is against you. We will all die. Case in point, last Christmas, I had 3 more brain surgeries. Christmas eve I was fine. Christmas day, I was in an incoherent state. My doctor said I would have been dead in another 24 hours without treatment. Try to knock out as many goals. You must stay focussed. Rewind to right after Sally and I were married. Our goal was to have a family. I didn't even realize this was my biggest goal in life. We just paid 10,000 dollars to do invitroferilization and they said we had twins. Sally and I went out and bought a crib. We were so excited. As we were putting it together, the doctors called and told us the hormone levels dropped- we lost the babies. That was one of the saddest days of my life. Sally walked out of the room and I stayed and finished putting the crib. We shut the door to the nursery for a month. We went to the doctors and after further testing, they said it would be 6 months before we could try again because I would have to wait until Lipitor cleared out of my system.

They said it was causing some problems. I looked at the doctor and said how much. The doctor said wait 6 months. I pressed him again and said how much to fix it. Then, he said 1,000 dollars to do ixsi which would solve the problem. You can't buy happiness, but it can solve many problems. That's the day I learned having money can help you achieve your big goals in life. $26,0000 later ($26,000 was the total we spent in 2 years), we had my daughter. We were on 2 teacher salaries just taking home around 48,000 a year with a mortgage payment of $1800 a month or 21,600 a year. Our parents did not give us any money towards invitroferilization. They gave support by giving us food. We had to decide how we could meet our goal of having a family. That's when I learned to cut everything from the budget. At one time, our grocery list was eggs, bread, and milk. By cutting everything from the budget, we were able to stay focused on our goals. We spent another $45,000 (over 3 years) to try to have a 2nd child. After the 9th time, the doctors said we would have to get an egg donor or adopt. We wanted our children to have our DNA, so we spent another 10,000 dollars with another doctor and got worse results. By having the money ($81,000), we were able to meet our goals. But, we wouldn't change a thing because we know we did not let money stand in our way of our goal to have a family. There is nothing in this life that is more valuable than my family. So, we had to save money and make sacrifices to meet our goal of having a family. I like to always think of it as a game: would I rather have my daughter or……….(eating out at a restaurant; buying a new car or TV; going on vacations, ect.). I don't need to keep up with the Joneses as long as I meet my goals. Spending money on the procedures to have my daughter was the most important goal in our life. We sacrificed and did whatever it took to achieve this goal. When you set goals in life and stay laser focused on those goals, you can achieve anything. After we stopped invitroferilization, we still used all the principles of savings and stayed on a tight budget. We set new goals. After Sally had a bad day at work, I asked her what is her number to quit. She said 1 million dollars (she has readjusted the number after we met our goal). Our goal switched from having a family to having the freedom to retire when we want to. 7 years later, we had a net worth of a million dollars.

Now we have money in our budget to do any goal in life. Since invitroferilization, we have spent over 200 days on cruise ships (8 times to Alaska, 3 times to Hawaii, 2 times to Europe, and too many times to count in the Caribbean). By having big goals in life, we were able to find many ways to save money and cut things out of the budget to save money. I always sweat the small bills and not worry about the big bills (we still pay all bills, but I try to eliminate all small bills/goals so we can set the money aside for bigger goals). You can nickel and dime yourself from being a millionaire. Goals keep you focused and not stray in a "million" different directions. So, I'll share 101 actions my wife and I did to reach our goal of being millionaires so you can become millionaires, too!

1. **No excuses** If you want something, do not let any excuse get in your way. Set a goal; figure out the steps to achieve your goal; and execute the steps to the goal. Make sure you talk to other people that have achieved your goal. If you want to play baseball, find some ex baseball players to talk to. In my class, I have guest speakers that achieved greatness in a field and explain what goals they set to achieve greatness. I have had a 2 time national

college soccer player, a college track star that runs professionally after college, an ex-baseball player, and an engineer that helped create the first high resolution camera used on the SR-1 spy plane. All the guest speakers talk about their goals and their determination to reach their goals. One speaker said she ran so much that she threw up after a practice. Would you do that? How bad do you want your goal? Another speaker was asked about when he had time to play playstation. He said, "There is no time for playstation during the season. It was practice, class and study tables." If you have a plan, you're more likely to achieve your goal. Let no excuse stand in your way of achieving your goal. You must have a great desire and determination to meet your goal.

2) **Have health insurance** As stated above, I had 6 brain surgeries when I was young. It would have been a financial strain on my family without insurance with the massive bills over 100,000. But insurance covered 100%. When I had my last 3 brain surgeries 2 years ago, my wife and I had no worries. We felt secure financially knowing that the surgeries were

covered. Also, we used insurance during invitroferilization. It paid some of the lab bills (not included in the $81,000). Also, we talked to the doctors and they worked with us on discounts and they tried to keep the costs down. Without insurance, medical bills can bankrupt you.

3) **Make goals as a family** We talk about our dreams and goals as a family- college, vacations, careers, and wants. By having a group goal, we can realize why we make certain sacrifices throughout the year. My daughter argues against my goal of spending $7,000 on a pinball machine, but we can't afford fries or we have to get a frito burrito at Taco Bell for a dollar. We just recently started eating out weekly. $5 a week. Even that is $5 x 52= $260 a year. I refuse to buy coffee or lunch out. A cup of coffee at Starbucks is $2 x 5 days a week x 52 weeks= $520 a year. A five dollar lunch x 5 days a week x 52 weeks =$1300 x 2 adults in a family and that would be $2600 a year. By having vacations as one of goals, we trade eating out for lunch for our goals. We are able to sacrifice the small things in life by seeing the bigger goal. For the past several years, we spent over $30,000 on vacations. We

have the most incredible summers. We all get a little depressed when we have to go back to school.

3) **Stay out of debt** If you have debt it robs you of your quality of life you could have. I don't go into debt for cars, college, or anything. Get the product you can afford. Early on we did no payments for 6 months on furniture. We had the money but we wanted to keep our bank account at a certain level. There is a risk of having to pay the interest if you are not able to pay it off in full. We were stupid. Even the no interest for 6 months is wrong. If an emergency comes up and you need the money for something else, you could get burned. Don't use payday loans places. In Ohio, the average payday loans have an interest rate of 667% according to cnbc.com. They rob you legally. Any loans/debt is dangerous. Case in point, we had the money to pay off my wife's student loans. I saved 10,000 by the time we were married. My dad said we should invest it and the stock market should make more than 8% and we make the difference. The stock market went up and down and by the time you pay taxes on the gain, the risk was not with the reward. Plus the stock market tanked in '08. Also, we bought one car that

we took a loan out for and we paid it off early. Also, Sally and I paid off our house in 10 years. Debt scares me. I have tried to stay out of debt at all costs- I have driven cars that we used duck tape to repair it. Also, Sally and I each found a way to get a Masters degree for free. If you are in debt, I'm scared for you and hope you get out of debt very fast. Cut all costs and get a 2nd job. I worked 70-80 hours the first 2 years we moved into this house because we were in too much debt. My 2 suggestions are that both of you should be working 70-80 hours and you should look up Dave Ramsey and follow his program. 99% of my beliefs about money and debt align with his philosophy. If you apply these 101 principles and your in debt, it will accelerate you to becoming debt free.

4) **Don't sweat the big stuff, sweat the small stuff**
I know I went over this above, but this is really one of the keys to becoming wealthy. Get focused on the major goals, and cut everything else out of your budget. When we were going through invitroferilization, we cut our grocery bill down to $20 a week. We only bought what is on sale and we never went down the snack aisle or pop aisle. Now

we buy a few snacks, but we still never buy potato chips, fritos, ect. We buy pop when there is a sale of 5 tp 6 dollars for a 24 pack and we try to limit only 1 pop a day. 10 years ago we ate out at Burger King for a treat. We had a buy one get one free coupon. The person at the register said we didn't have to ring it up separately. What the cashier did was give us 2 chicken sandwiches for free and charged us for 2 whoppers. The cashier said I gave you 2 sandwiches for free. The error was 41 cents. I got the manager and the manager did not understand the Math after I did it on a piece of paper. Finally he got frustrated and said how much do we owe you. I said 41 cents and he laughed and said just give him the money. We monitor any monthly bills and try to get them as low as possible. I constantly reduce our cable, alarm, and gas bill. Just by looking around at other companies or asking to lower the bill to keep you as a customer, usually, you can get your bill lowered. Now saying that, I would not have a cell phone or cable until I was out of debt including my house. Eliminate monthly bills

5) **Have a savings account** By having a savings account, you can afford to solve problems when they

enter your life. Now saying that, I still don't just write checks to people when we have a problem. I find lower cost solutions. But the savings account is a sense of security. We had to have $10,000 to do invitroferilization. The hard deck we established not to go below was 10,000. It gave us a great sense of security. We had to cut a lot of corners to keep it at that, but we never had to stop our goals because of monetary reasons. By having a large savings, some places will give you a discount if you pay in full. Our orthodontist gave us a discount to pay in full.

6) **7 degrees from having a friend fix the problem cheaper**. Everybody always thinks there are only one or two solutions to fix a problem. When your back is up against the wall and your goal is life or death, you get very creative on how to solve a problem. You would ask everybody you know if they could help you or if they knew of anybody that could help you. So the real question is what are you willing to do to achieve your goal. For instance, we just moved into a house and we couldn't afford to fix the O2 sensor on my wife's car. My brother in law didn't have time to fix the car. My wife refused to ask one of her coworkers to ask her husband to help me. I

went out and replaced it myself using the internet. She had to take it to a shop and they charged 30 dollars to frighten the sensor (saved $140). Another car job was too big. Sally didn't want to ask her friend again. So, I left the hood up and the part and directions on how to fix it on the engine. She didn't want me to touch the car so she got her coworkers husband to fix the car. Now, I have a friend's husband that will fix any problem on the car except the engine and transmission for $30 to 50 dollars. I know my friend from highschool for insurance, a neighbor that sells cars, my brother-in-law for heating and air conditioning, a friend's tax preparer, and several people that service and buy arcade machines. We do all of the house cleaning and lawn service ourselves. When something breaks or we need a service, I try to find a cheaper method of fixing by means of having a friend or a friend of a friend fix the problem for pennies on the dollar. We are 7 people away from saving tons of money!

7) **Don't be afraid to ask for a discount** Many times, I will ask if there are any additional discounts. I usually play the teacher card. One time my wife and I were buying tires and I asked the sales

manager if there were any discounts for teachers. My wife rolls her eyes at me. But he said he could knock off a hundred dollars. Norwegian used to give discounts for unions. I asked if there were any discounts for teachers. Also, if you're a repeat customer, I always ask if there are discounts. One tour in Alaska took off 100 dollars off the price of the tour because we went on it before with them. I asked sears one time about discounts and they got 4 new 80,000 miles tires for $429 when the sale price was $550. I asked if he could do better than that. Also we got $25 a month to shop at sears as a shop your way rewards member. I would make sure not to go over $25. That bought a lot of socks, jeans and underwear.

8) **Don't eat out** Americans waste more money eating out. The average American family spends $3000 dollars a year eating out. Back about 16 years ago, Arby's would do the 5 for 5. One Christmas, I told my friend I got Sally 5 gifts and I paid for gift wrapping. He was shocked. Then, he laughed when I told him it was Arby's 5 for $5 dollars. When we first got married, we spent 10 dollars a week to eat out (I know, I cringe to think how much money we were

wasting a year ($520) when we really couldn't afford to be wasting money). Now my wife would jump at $10 a week eating out. 10 x 52 = $520 dollars we were wasting that first year of marriage. Now we spend 5 dollars a week to eat out ($260 a year).
 Even though we have over a million dollars, I'd rather buy a pinball machine for $6000 or go on vacations than eat out.

9) **2nd Job** After college, people feel entitled not to pay off their debt or want to set an extreme goal and work really hard at it. When we first got married, I quit a teaching job in the inner city due to the stress.
 In order to make the house payment, both of us had to get 2nd jobs. I worked 70 to 80 hours for 2 years.
 My wife had a full time teaching job, a second job, and was going to grad school to get her masters.
 She Hates the JCpenny's because they kept messing up her schedule and scheduling her when she couldn't work. She had a meeting with the manager and blew up at the manager. At my part time job, I w as robbed at gunpoint at Blockbuster. I asked if I could have the next shift off and they said yes, but unpaid. I showed up to work the next night.
 At another part time job, I was a telemarketing

manager at a cemetery. There were just 2 to three of us. Everybody quit, so I was working shifts by myself. One night leaving the cemetery, I was runned off the road. The car was trying to crash into me because I was mistaken for the cleaning lady. She was going through a divorce and her husband wanted to kill her because he didn't want to pay for alimony. For 3 weeks after that, I had a police escort to my car every night. When you make stupid financial decisions like buying a house when you couldn't afford it, you get trapped into working at jobs you don't like. I felt like a slave to my house payment. I still remember the night I got my full time teaching job I have now, we celebrated with 2 bottles of wine just sitting in our house that we could now afford and enjoy.

10) **Using your benefits at your job to make purchases**

My wife could get a 20 percent discount on furniture from a department star she worked for as her 2nd job. The only problem was the delivery people would deliver the furniture scratched up. We went to the local furniture store and asked the store manager if he could match my wife's employee discount. He said yes (Sally worked with the manager's wife at her second job). We furnished our whole house that way. Of course I always asked for free delivery. The manager said one time that he couldn't pay a delivery driver to deliver the order because he was only making 6 dollars off the sale. So I agreed to help move in the pieces of furniture if he delivered it on his way home. We Saved 1000's of dollars furnishing our home this way. You buy the best furniture that you like, but you buy it near wholesale prices. Also, you always must have the money for your purchases. Never take financing. Even at 0% financing, the store is betting on you having a late payment or after the period is up, you're not able to pay off the item. In most cases, they will charge you interest from day one.

11) Don't take out car loans

Buy a car you can pay cash for. We have only had one car loan since we were married (22 years). The first car we bought was on it's last leg at one of those buy here pay here lots . The car had some problems, but we only paid $1500 because I was in grad school. My brother-in-law fixed the few things that were wrong with it (7 degrees from solving any problem). It ran for 2 years,and we sold it to my brother in law for $850. The cost to buy the car per month was only paid $27. This is a lot cheaper than a new car payment that most people can't afford.

Since we drove a lot of mileage we did not go with a lease ever when buying a car. The fees with the payments make it one of the most expensive ways to operate a car. In case you're wondering, we did buy a new Honda Civic in 09. The next door neighbor worked there and told us of an internet salie at the end of the year where we purchased the car for around $ 15,478. The next new car we got is due to the mistake of the operator. We called the car dealership and they said they were offering $2000 on a drive, push, drag event. We got down to the dealership. I'm surprised the car's transmission made it. We were on borrowed time. The manager said the operator missed quoted us. He said if he offered the $2000 with the discounts, it would be below invoice. He said he wanted to make it right and offered a $100 dollars above invoice. He showed us the invoice. We drove it home that day without even test driving it. The manager said,

"Atleast, I'll make a little on sale off the loan." I responded, "We're paying with a check."

12) Pay off your mortgage in 10-11 years Most people say take a thirty year fixed rate for your mortgage. A few say a 15 year fix rate is better because you're going to be out of debt faster. 15 years is too long for me. In between invitroferilization, we would still be saving like crazy. We would have a pile of cash that we would apply to the principal of our mortgage. This leads me to my next point. Make sure your mortgage company applies it to principal. On one of the principal reductions that we did, the mortgage representative just applied the 20,000 to our payments. No new payments were due for the next few years. This does not help you with interest. I checked on the principal and it was not lowered by 20,000. I called up the mortgage company. At first, they said don't worry. There is not much difference in savings. I call B.S. I talked to the manager and I told him I was on a recorded line. I explained to them that they should be able to look up the call and hear that I said principal reduction. After a few days, the mortgage company called back and apologized for their mistake and corrected their error. According to businessinsider.com, the average millionaire pays off their house in 11 years. If you have a goal (a goal of becoming a millionaire), then start behaving like one! Pay off your house in 10-11 years.

13) **Don't have cable/satellite** Average cable in America according to decisiondata.org in March 2020 was 217 dollars. You multiply that by 12 months and the cost is $2604. You might say my bill is not nearly that much. Maybe, it's only $70. That is $840 dollars a year. When we had a goal of invitroferilization, that was way too much. If I wanted to really watch a football game I would go over to my parents or friend's to watch it. I also would go to a bar, buy a pop and watch the game. $2 for Coke is cheaper than paying $130 (That's what we pay for 100meg of internet, cable and phone). Rabbit ears are $15 in some stores. In ten years, the average American spends $26,040 on cable. How big of a goal is it for you to have cable? Do you realize all the things $26,040 buys you. For us, we suffered about 12 years without cable, but I have my daughter! Having my daughter is a better goal than watching some show on cable anyday.

14) **Don't have cell phones** Just after we paid off our house, we purchased a cell phone (a burn phone). It wasn't until we were well over a million dollars did we buy a regular cell phone with a cell phone carrier- Spectrum. Spectrum is only 14 dollars a month no hidden taxes or fees. $14 x 12months is $168 dollars a year x 3 people in my family = $504 dollars per year. Plus the Spectrum phones were $150 dollars a piece. Never roll the cost of a new cell phone into your monthly payment. If you can't afford to buy the phone you want, then buy a cheaper one or don't buy a new one at all. Having a cell phone is a pet peeve of mine. I feel most people don't need them and they can save the monthly bill of $70 per month or $840 dollars a year. This is more expensive than my families' three cell phone plans put together. However, a burn phone smart plan is $125 a year (tracfone). This is inexpensive but very limited minutes, texts and data. Personally, I would recommend a land line which would be $15-$30 a month ($180 a year). And if you're in debt (even a car payment or a mortgage), I would recommend a second job and no cell phone. If you work all the time, you really don't have anytime to play on a cell

phone. Monthly bills drive me crazy. I try to reduce them down as small as possible or eliminate them all together. Don't take on debt by having the cost of the cell phone put on monthly installment plains in your bill. Worst yet, I have heard of people leasing their phone/future. If you can't afford to buy the phone outright from savings, don't buy it.

15) **Don't buy new clothes for your kids** My daughter does not remember any of the clothes she wore from the ages 0-6. We were still going through in vitro and clothes were not in the budget. My parents wanted to help, so they bought the used clothes from my sister that she was selling and gave them to us. We did buy one outfit when she was 3 months old for our first family picture.   The average amount in America spent on kids for clothing from 0-17 years of age is $13,260. You Can buy a car for that. As my daughter has gotten older, we have gotten new clothes because she has caught up to my niece. And yes my mom treats my daughter to most of her clothes. That's one of the biggest ways they help out. My mom knows I would buy her used clothes and shoes now. My parents won't give us money, but they help us out in other ways. Clothing

was the one area we asked for help when we were going through everything. My mom will buy my daughter clothes sometimes and my dad will always buy us a drink. Family time is important!

16) **Buy cheap formula** I will start this paragraph out by saying this in my opinion backed up with the data of my daughter. Sally did not feel comfortable breastfeeding. One misleading fact that our invitroferilization doctor pointed out that there were the same amount of bottle fed and breastfed students entering ivy league schools (a report he saw back around 2006). And if you decide to breastfeed, you have to watch your diet very closely. We opted to go with a formula from Sam's club that has DHA. We kept her in a bottle for seven months because we were scared to make the jump to solid foods. Today, she is in the top of her class in middle school and has skipped 2 grades in Math. She has scored perfect scores on the OST/OGT test in Math and scores in the top bracket in Reading. But I always point out to her that the average millionaire's GPA is below 3.0 for college. I stress to her, it's about the hard work. But, she just replies that her goal is to get scholarships for college and bank her 529 for

herself(you can withdraw the amount of the scholarship tax free from the 529). She is working very hard in school to achieve this goal. It's amazing how hard you will work when you want to achieve your goals.

17) **Buy cheap diapers** We bought the cheapest diapers that we could find which were Sam's Diapers (Today's prices-$13.98 for 108 newborn diapers 12 cents per diaper vs $39.99 for 186 pampers at Target 21 cents per diaper. That could be around $100 a month. We just changed her when she cried and the cheaper diapers worked fine. Really, why do people spend so much money on diapers when they just hold……

18) **Don't exchange gifts with your spouse** the first christmas while we're dating. My wife gave me several presents that I didn't like and I returned all the presents except for a Far Side mug which I still use to this day. After that we don't exchange gifts. If we want something now that we're married we just discuss it with the other person - budget meeting. Why do people spend money to surprise their spouse when given the chance and the same amount of money your spouse probably wouldn't have picked

that gift you gave as the first gift. Now if it's June and I want something that she thinks is ridiculous and a waste of money, I'll say it's my Christmas/ birthday gift. Why would you spend money on something your spouse does not know of. Any major purchase (any purchase over $1) we discuss. You might think that's stupid, but are you and your spouse millionaires that spent over 30,000 on vacations last year. Keep nickeling and diming yourself from being rich.

19) **Buy children gifts for the first five years at the dollar store**

Most children are more interested in the box than the toys as the old joke goes. My daughter does not remember what she got from Christmas for the first five years of her life, but she remembers all the places we have traveled and the time we spent together. Spending time with your children is the most important thing to improve their future. They will be better prepared for school. We would play tons of board games. The Dollar Store or 5 and Below were the 2 stores we shopped at for her birthday and Christmas for the first five years because we had a goal of having another child. Still to this day we don't spend more than $25 dollars on

X-mas (This past X-mas we bought her a real cell phone for $150. That was birthday and Christmas all rolled into one). She still survives on 1 gig of data for her phone, but she connects to wi-fi to save her data. Spectrum is only $14 a month for unlimited talk, text, and 1 gig of data. Do you want a paid off house or do you want to be selling a bunch of toys at a garage sale?

20) **No big children birthday parties** My daughter only has one big birthday party at a splash park with pizza and cake. The average birthday cake is $25 dollars and plates and napkins. We had Papa John's pizza 5 x $10= $50+$25+ party favors/Balloons= $100 x13= $1,300. We always make homemade cakes now. My mother actually made homemade icing and had the grand kids their own cake which you could do for a party with a cake mix for around $1.50 plus icing $1.60. For around $3-$4, you can have a cake vs $25. Now she usually has friends over and we get pizza. The average birthday cost in America is $478.78. This is due to people having at some event place where you have everybody do a fun activity and they host the party after. $478 x 10

=$4780 or close to $5000 in 10 years of kids birthdays. And that's only if you have one kid!

21) **Buy season passes** This is my best advice. We have had amusement park passes since my daughter's been born (I have a Kings island season pass since 1984). Passes are inexpensive ways to have a great time with little cost. One year my daughter and I went to Kings Island 55. The passes were $80. When you pay less than 2dollars a time to go to an amusement park it's worth the money. We have certain rules for amusement parks: no gift shops, no food, no drink, and no dining upgrade to your season pass. We get water in the park and we pack pop and lunch in the car. The only place that charges for a cup of tap water is Canada's Wonderland owned by Cedar Fair. Don't worry, I spoke to a manager who was American. He thought the rule was crazy and got us 3 cups of water. He said the cost was to cover the cost of the cup.

Remember, if you're in any debt (including a mortgage) skip this step until you are completely debt free. Family time is important, but you can always play board games at home until you pay off your debts.

22) **Be aware of extended warranties. I** don't buy extended warranties because you rarely use them. The profit margins on extended warranties is about 50 percent according to forbes.com. According to Google, 47% of the people buy extended warranties. In general 50% of the cost of warranties goes directly back to the company that is selling the extended warranty. It would be better for you to take the money and put it into your bank account and use it for any repairs on the item. You would come out ahead.

23) **Invest on a regular basis beyond 401 k and pension** Most people are content to wait to retire when social security is available or when they can start collecting a pension. 10 years ago, my wife had a bad day at work. We Had a drink and I asked her how much it would take for us to stop working. She said 1 million dollars (since then it has been changed because our goals have changed in life). We invest in our work 401k (State Teacher Retirement System), we max out our Roth IRA's, and then we invest the rest of our money into a regular mutual fund like an index 500 fund. The rule of 72 = (years to double = 72/ interest rate).

An interest rate of 10% would take you 7.2 years to double your money (72/10=7.2 years). According to cnbc.com, 401k millionaires were up 35% in the year 2020 (more than 180,000 millionaires). Are you fully contributing to your 401 k up to the match? You should!

24) **Roth IRA's** Most people are content to wait to retire when social security is available or when they can start collecting a pension. Don't rely on social security or pensions. You decide when you retire. You set your goal when you want to retire. I want to retire by 55. What makes Roth IRA different from pensions and mutual funds outside of a Roth is the Roth IRA grows tax free. In a mutual fund you take taxed money to invest and you pay taxes on the growth. In a pension you invest pre tax dollars and invest it into the pension. You pay taxes when you take it out of the pension. On the Roth IRA you pay no taxes on anything you take out as long as you're 59.5. You can take out your original investment anytime without penalty. If you invest the max in your Roth from 20 to 63 at an average rate return of 7%, you would have over 1.59 million dollars at a 28% tax bracket, you would have 1.14 million. If you invest it

in a Roth, you would have paid only 72,000 in taxes instead of paying 450,000 dollars in pension. Also to meet my goal of retiring at the age of 55, my wife and I are putting money into a regular mutual fund that we can pull from the ages 55-59 ½.

25) **Try to fix your own problem before calling a handyman** I usually find out how much the repair man will charge. I find how much teh parts cost. If most of the expense is in labor I try to fix it myself. If I can't find how to fix it, I'll start calling friends and ask if anybody knows how to fix it or knows anybody that can fix it. This will save on the cost of labor. On my last fix (my lawn mower), it wouldn't start, so my wife said let's just get a new one. My nephew used to work on lawn mowers and used to say they were easy to fix. This gave me confidence to look on youtube on how to fix it. I had to take apart the lawn mower and clean the carburetor. After 1 hour, I had it fixed and put back together. It saved me $200-$300.
26) **Don't go into debt to pay for college**   There are lots of websites they will find. The one that we have looked at is https://myscholly.com/ . My daughter's job (5 hours a week) her junior and senior

year is to apply for scholarships. We have already met one of the admissions persons that deal with scholarships at Bowling Green State University. We are involved in her school work and always placed an importance on school. She is one of the top students in her middle school. She skipped to grades in Math and she got a perfect score on the State test twice before. I told her from elementary that we would pay for 3 years of college and her wedding. She was motivated to get a full ride to college and withdraw the money out of her 529 tax free to her bank account. She strived to be the best at everything when she started to play select soccer in third grade. If you were on time for practice, you were 10 minutes late. The effort in soccer rolled over into her education. Now, my wife and I were not as smart as that and we got full rides on our Masters degree. I wanted to go back to college and get a Masters in Education because I couldn't find any work as a health and safety inspector. So, I asked my parents to pay for a master in Education. They said no. So, I knew I didn't want to go into debt for school. I called around to several schools. Wright State said they have a masters program and I could qualify for a minority scholarship/fellowship. Now as a white male, I was intrigued. They said I could get a scholarship for being a male in elementary. My wife 2 years later got a scholarship for being a female in Science (Environmental Science Masters). We both got a full ride to college because we asked around. We just got married and we were still messing around with my wife's student loan and knew we didn't want any more debt. If you have a goal and enough desire, you can achieve anything.

27) **I have a guy** I hate to pay full retail on repairs. So most situations I have a guy that will fix things for 30-50 dollars plus parts. Over the years, when something breaks we ask around and find people that do side work for fixes on a variety of things for a fraction of the cost than it would be to call a repair guy or take it to the shop. Also, check with friends to see if they know how to fix the problem or if they know anybody on the side that can fix the problem. Usually by going with a person instead of a company for fixes, I can save 50% or more. Also, check with people at church, work, friends, and social network to find a person to solve your problem.

28) **No vacations** If you have debt, you should use all of your income to get out of debt. This Includes your house and car loans. Once you have no debt payments, you can invest and save a lot faster. Americans spend $2000 a year on average on vacations. In 10 years that is 20,0000. That money could be to pay off a lot of debt or used to invest in a Roth IRA or mutual funds. We did not vacation until we had our house paid off and finished going through Invitro. We did go on a few vacations that my parents took us on. But we did turn down a free vacation while going through invitroferilization, because we had a bigger goal in life- having a family. Once we were out of debt 10 years ago, we started vacationing. We have been on cruise ships more than 200 days as a family; we have been to Europe, Canada, Mexico, Caribbean, Alaska, and Hawaii. There is plenty of time to vacation after you are completely debt free as long as you set it as a goal!!!

29) **No eating out at work** At our work, most people eat out once or twice a week. If we do that, 37 weeks times $5= $185 a year. In 5 years, tha't $1000. What goals can you achieve with $1000? I never hear anybody saying they want to set a goal of eating

out. Yes, you will have to pack. But, we pack for under a dollar per person in my family. We buy whole hams on sale, slice them and freeze them. We buy yogurt for 40 cents and we have a reverse osmosis system at home for water. Usually have a cup of coffee (K-cup walmart 28 cents), a yogurt (40 cents) and a sandwich (24 cents = a total of 92 cents a day). This is a savings of $24.08 per week per person or around $1252 a year ($2504 for a couple). You could buy a new car with cash ($25,000 in 10 years), if you just pack your lunch. What are your goals in life!

30) **Don't buy crap because it goes to a good cause- donate directly**

At one of my 2nd jobs, I worked for a telemarketing firm that raised money for special olympics and other organizations. On the average sale they would donate $4-$8. I would make $6 to $10 on the sale. This was my wife's least favorite part time job. Most organizations only use about 10% of the sale to the cause. Also, most charitable organizations have a large overhead and administration. It's better to donate a few dollars to the organization directly or cause than going through a fundraiser. The best fundraiser the school I worked at was a walkathon where the school received 100 percent of the profits minus a few prizes given out. These are the type of fundraisers to look for and get behind. I love walkathons!!!!

31) **Be content** Never worry about other people's goals. I never tried to keep up with Jones. I wanted to be the Jonese. By staying out of debt, paying off our house, and keeping our goals in focus, we were able to meet our goals. Now we can buy or have the money to do what we want. But we still have goals and meetings to set our goals. We have discussions about money and whether the activity/item is worth the money. We still have financial goals that we are still focused on achieving. That's why we still eat $1 Tacos when we need to eat out somewhere and we always get water. When my daughter complains, I always tell her she can use her birthday money to buy whatever she wants. She always says no because she saves her money to go to the football games at school and buy a snack.

32) **Don't carry balances on credit cards** My belief is only buy what you can afford (if you don't have the money, don't buy it). One of the biggest

fights my wife and I had was after our honeymoon. I found out she just carried a balance on a credit card (around a $1 in interest). She left the room and said, "I'll take you for half of everything." I responded back with "Minus the 10,000 you owe me because I'm paying off your loans." She got right into my face and I realized from that day on, it was our money. Credit cards are like snakes, eventually you get bitten and pay the price (interest) even if you pay the bill off every month.

33) **Don't spend money you don't have** If you don't have the money, don't buy it. Don't use: no money done, no payments, no interest for. All of these are gimmicks for stores to get you to spend money that you don't have and then they tax on interest/ fees when you're unable/ break the terms of the agreement. The biggest fight we had was right after the honeymoon. I opened my wife's credit card and realized that she had paid interest because she didn't have enough money right before the wedding. She yelled during the fight "I'll take you for ½ of everything." I responded back minus the 10,000 dollars of mine that I used to pay off the loans." After that, we combined finances and bills. By combining

our finances we are able to achieve goals we have in common.

34) **Groceries** Any recurring weekly/monthly bill you should get it as low as possible. When we were first married, we spent $20 dollars a week on groceries. No snacks and only buy what's on sale. Her parents had cattle, so we could get free meat, but we would go up every other weekend to help out on the farm. I have banded a few bulls in my day! They called us to come up one night at 12 midnight because the cows got out. Well worth it for the free meat. We buy the cheap bread and only buy meat in whole blocks because it's ½ the price to slice it yourself. If it's a name brand, it's not on our grocery list. Store brand only. Our meat was so thin, Sally used to call ham sandwiches,- scamswitches . Also, Stock up on frozen food when it goes on sale- and you have to know the difference of sale price and the lowest sale price. My wife still says something is on sale and I'll reply back that it's not on sale. It could be lower. Even after my daughter was born, we still stick to under $100 per month for groceries. Sally does bake a lot of things from scratch. Also, we learned when certain things go on sale. I love blueberry muffins. I

know blueberries go on sale in the first part of June and I stock up on them then for the year. Skip the snack and frozen meal aisle. Make the meals yourself. It's a lot cheaper.

35) **Insurance** Find an insurance broker. They can shop around for the cheapest insurance. I found my friend from highschool. He gives me the lowest rates possible because they shop around (I thought it was because we were friends but he says he does it for everyone). Once we could afford to buy a new car with cash (we keep an emergency fund large enough to buy a new car), we lowered our car insurance to collusion only because we could save $1000 a year. With depreciation, older cars are not worth having full coverage on them. If you get into an accident, you can replace your $2000 dollar car with another $2000 car. But if you do the Math, it is always better to go with liability when you buy 20,000 cars and don't get into accidents. With an inexpensive used car, I would put liability only on it because it's not worth the extra money for insurance on $1,000-$3,000. We just recently switched the coverage from full to collusion in the past few years. After I did the Math, I could buy a Honda Civic for $19,000 new.

The full coverage insurance is around $1000 (to keep it simple). In 7 years, I spent $7,000 on insurance. The car according to Kelly Blue Book in my area would bring $6,300. After 7 year of saving $1,000 dollars a year (total of $7,000), I could replace my car if I got into an accident and walk away with $700 savings. Sally, my wife, would like to have full coverage for the sense of security, but she can't argue with Math!

36) **Don't go down the snack aisle** Our grocery budget during invitroferilization was $20. We had no money for snacks except for 1 bag of pretzels for 99 cents. We never buy snacks and still don't buy potato chips, Duritos, ect. We buy healthy snacks like bananas or apples. One time, I kept the family out too late at Red Rock Canyon in Vegas.

 Everybody was sunburned and hangry. I stopped by the grocery store and bought the family size of Doritos and a dozen donuts. We still talk about that night. We just went back to Las Vegas so my daughter could jump out of the Stratosphere. Las Vegas is my wife's least favorite place to go. So, I recreated Dorito's and day old donuts from the grocery store. This time she said we could afford the

99 cents for 3 donuts for our breakfast each day. I agreed reluctantly. Atleast, she did not want to pay full price for fresh donuts.

37) **No pets** According to google, it costs $1400 to $1836 dollars a year to care for a dog/cat after food/vet bills (153 dollars a month according to thrillist.com). Even a fish tank cost $116 annually to run electricity for lights and filters per year. Even though pets provide emotional support to our lives, the cost to own them most people can't afford. I have had hermit crabs all my life. No lights or heat lamps run $15 a year in food. Owning a dog for ten years at $14,000 or owning a car, I would choose a car or apply it towards debt or down payment for a house. After 30 years, that is $42,000 or 2 new vehicles, a boat, or so many other goals that you could have achieved!

38) **No expensive shoes** I see in school, kids that say they can't afford school supplies, but have a $65 to $85 pair of shoes (psychologytoday.com). Most people wear shoes as status symbols. I have never paid over $50 dollars for a pair of my shoes- Nike Air Monarchs 3. Most people don't even have savings of $1000 (58% of Americans - Fianceyahoo.com) have

a pair of shoes worth more than $100 (50% of men and 68% of women). Why would you have 10% of your wealth or 20% of your wealth if married tied up in shoes. Is that a smart investment? On a recent family trip on Frontier Airlines, a college student a row up from us was bragging to her brother about how she was going to spend $400 dollars on shoes. She said the Nike stores out west have the newer styles. She was so eager to get the newest style of Nikes so she could make her friends jealous. If she would invest the $400 in the S&P 500 at the average rate of 12% until she was 65 (43 years), the $400 dollars would turn into $52,291.97. That is a lot of money to impress people you probably won't even be in touch with when you are 65 years old.

39) **Efficient gas cars** Gas efficient cars can save #3200 per year according to consumer reports. I drive a 2009 Honda civic 2009 that stills get 35 miles per gallon. Also, I like Hondas because they are easy to work on. I can change the spark plugs and most things myself. I Have a friend that can fix most things in under a ½ hour. He usually charges me $40-$50 per job. I also found a garage near me that will charge a flat rate if I bring in the part. By having

fuel efficient cars, it does not stress you out every time you pull up at the pump.

40) **Have a good paying job** If you don't have a good paying job, pick another job. When I first got out of college, a health and safety inspector job salary was 16,000 in myrtle beach. I turned it down because my wife was offered 26,000 as a starting teacher. I wanted to go back, so I found a minority fellowship- males in elementary. In 10 years, the difference is $100,000. That's a lot of money to stick in a job that is low paying even if you enjoy it. It's best to have both- a high paying job that you like. If you don't feel like you have a high enough paying job,set a goal for a career change and make it happen. I had a job over 16,500 to become a health inspector back in 1997. That was too low. What did I do? I figured I could make more as a teacher than I could as a Health and Safety Inspector. I switched careers. When I did this, I found a way to do it debt free (a full scholarship/fellowship- males in elementary and my wife got a full scholarship based on being a female in Science).

41) **Plant all your trees and shrubs** When you plant your own bushes and trees, you pay a fraction

of the price. We had a family member that spent over 20,000 on their yard because they hired one of the best landscapers. I have the same yard for around $1000 because I planted all my trees and shrubbery myself. I copied my mom's plan and made tweaks to her plan. Now, we have one of the nicest yards in the neighborhood. Also, you should do all your own mulching and weeding. Now, we do have a lawn guy- say what???? Are You throwing money away Scott? No. I bargain with the lawn people. I tell the landscapers the price I could buy the Scott's 4 step bags at Lowes and that is the max budget I'm willing to spend on my lawn. He asked me how much I was spending. After I told him, he said, "What would you say if I could price match the price." It never hurts to ask for a lower price or tell people this is my budget for this.   You do have to be willing to walk away from bad deals. We have been getting this great rate for the past 4 years, because I just asked a simple question.

42) **Cut your own grass** Things you're able to do physically, you should. Average cost for grass service in the U.S. is $30-$80 per visit depending on size and service. That's $840 to $2240 per year. It's

good exercise and it saves money. Two goals accomplished with one action. It's a win, win.

43) **Paint your own house** I watched the painters in my house touch up our house when we first moved in. I learned a few quick tips. It was going to cost $2400 to paint the inside of the house. The paint cost $400 for lifetime guarantee paint. I painted every night for 1 week from 6P.M. til 2A.M. With the money we saved I bought a Star Wars Arcade machine for $800 (back then the cost was double). Now it's worth $4000. I saved money and got an awesome arcade machine for my man cave. Side note it took 5 guys to get the machine downstairs and I didn't realize the screen was high voltage. A video game repair guy said if one of us would have touched the back part of the screen, we would have been shot across the room. Thank God nobody got hurt.

44) **No smoking** Besides the health risks, smoking is very costly.

The National Cancer Institute states the average cost of a pack of cigarettes is $6.28 (thebalance.com). So, if you smoke a pack-a-day it would cost you $188 per month or $2,292 per year. In ten years, smoking would cost you $22,920. You can buy a new car for that or a down payment on a house for not smoking. Besides the initial money, you have an average increase of your health insurance of 50% in 40 states. According to cdc.gov, smoking shortens 10 years off your life expectancy. The cost is crazy and you shorten your life. Why would you smoke?

45) **Don't buy the newest TV or Game system** I always wait a few years to buy a TV or a game system. My newest TV is 10 years old and I bought my new game system 5 years after it came out. I had reward points at Toys R us.and bought my PS4 for no money on the last day they let you use them before they went out of business. I bought older games that were $25 and below. You can save half the price on a game system if you wait 3-5 years after they come out. Same with TV's.   They lose 30-50% of their value after their first year (Software Engineer at Red Hat). We don't replace TV's unless they break. I have one Tube TV I still use by my pool table because I'm content not to have the newest gadgets. And I go a step further by saying you shouldn't buy any game system or any electronics if you are in debt.

46) Look for free- free concerts, free movies library, or free chicken sandwich on Chick-fil-a day I constantly look for free stuff to do. On an average year in Ohio, I will see 3-6 free concerts. A lot of cities will have free concerts around holidays- usually 80's groups. Casinos also have free concerts. They expect that you will drop several dollars into the slots, but I don't. I grab my free pop and stand in line. Also, most free concerts are general admission. So if you get there early, you can get a front row seat to a concert for free. My wife stopped going to these after I started waiting out longer than 12 hours. Libraries offer free movies and you can request them in most libraries so it's cheaper than on-demand or Redbox. The last freebee is my favorite. Cow Appreciation Day at Chick-fe-la. You dress up like a cow or put on a cow hat and you get one free entree. You used to get a whole value meal. Chick-fe-la please bring back the free value meal for dressing up in a full cow costume on Cow appreciation day. There are 5 Chick-fe-la's close to me, so score!!!!

47) Use air conditioning in the car- surprising it is more efficient than the windows down This one might surprise you. We did a test about 20 years ago with 2 cars. We did a 2 tank study. Each car did one take with the windows down and another tank of gas with the windows up and the air condition on. Both cars came back with surprising results. The cars with the windows up and the air conditioner on had better gas mileage by several miles per gallon. Ever since then, we use the air conditioner at all times driving now.

48) **Clean your own house**   Some people feel entitled to have somebody cleanup after them once they become middle class. They feel tired and feel like they have no time to spend with the family are common excuses to hire a housekeeper. The average housekeeper makes $40-$80. If you have your house cleaned weekly it would cost (52 weeks times $60) $3,120. Even if you get your house cleaned every 2 weeks, it would cost (26 weeks x$60) = $1,560. In our family everybody takes ownership in the cleaning. We all are cleaning something or vacuuming or working in the yard. When we all are cleaning, nobody feels like they are carrying an unfair share of the housework.

49) **Family time is best sitting around and talking**
My favorite memories of family are sitting around and talking. From family reunions on a farm to sitting around a table watching Nascar, having a beer with my mom and dad or being trapped in a car for 17 hours and having to listen to each other. No matter what, all my favorite memories are talking to family. The places where you talk does not matter. The place can be at home, in a car, at a restaurant, or around a table. Sharing stories and your thoughts can be so powerful and it doesn't cost a thing. Most families don't spend enough time these days bonding like this.

50) **Revisit goals to make sure they are still everybody's goals** We are constantly looking at our main goals for our family to make sure we are placing our energy in life in the proper place. We have had goals as small as getting a car to as big as a new house to a baby to vacations. Set your goal; write it down; put steps in place to achieve your goal; constantly look at your steps to make sure you're still on track to achieve your goal!

51) **Family vote** Besides having family goals, we have a family vote system to make daily decisions.

Some decisions are just my wife and I. Other decisions we take are a family vote where my daughter gets a vote too. On all major money decisions, my wife and I make a unified decision. We don't proceed with the transaction/purchase unless we both agree. If I grab a dollar taco, I call home and give her a heads up so her and Megan can go get one and vice versa. We take a family vote if we are going somewhere. If people don't want to go, we usually don't stop people from doing what they want. I enjoy concerts, but my wife doesn't anymore, so I go with friends. I always ask her before purchasing tickets. We take family votes on vacations, eating out ($1 taco or $5 pizza) and doing things. Also, this teaches my daughter about fairness. When she wants to watch something on T.V. at the same time I'm watching something, I don't get into an argument. I simply say I can cut you in on the cable bill this month if you want to pay a third. I'll go to the bank and take it out of your bank account. It stops her from arguing and teaches her a valuable lesson.

52) **No movie theatres**   The average cost for a movie theatre is $9. Movies around Ohio can range from $5.50 (for special weekly rate) to 15. At $5.50

for a family of 4, it would be $22. Average concessions for 2019 was $4.46 per person (total for family of 4 is $17.84) according to AMC. By the time you get tickets and concessions it would be close to $40. You do that 4 times a year and that's $160. That is a lot of money to spend on movies when you can get free movies to watch at the library or rent it at RedBox for $1.75.

53) **No DVD's /Blue-rays** The average dvd movie cost $13. Most people brag about how many dvds they have. How many people have the The Star Wars or Harry Potter series on dvd. People have wasted $1000 on dvds. If you really want to watch a series, get it from the library or netflix. Binge watch it during the trial period and you don';t have any costs. We did that with Star Wars: The Mandalorian on Disney. USAtoday.com says Americans spend 18,000 a year on non essential spending. Over 10 years, that is 180,000-a house. Cut out non essentials for 10 years and buy a house for yourself with cash!!

54) **The Library** As stated above, buying books, dvd's, and downloading can be very costly (over $100 annually). You can go to the library, borrow it

and return it for free. Most of the time you don't watch movies over and over. You can download songs from libraries. You can get ebooks. Some libraries even have video games. So before you go out and buy the newest dvd or download the newest song, stop by your library and save yourself around $100 a year.

55) **No gym membership/ run outside** An average gym membership costs $40 a month or $360 a year (cnbc.com). Some places offer $10 a month or $120 a year. I went into a gym and spoke to a personal trainer and asked them which machines would help me lose weight. They had a huge room filled with machines and he pointed at the treadmill and the elliptical machine. He said all the other machines would be for building muscle or toning. I asked what is the difference from running outside and the treadmill. He said if you are just trying to lose weight, just run outside. Save yourself $120 a year or $1,200 over 10 years by running outside. Yes it can get cold during the winter and hot during the summer, but isn't $1,200 worth it. Also, you might not need the gym anymore since you don't eat out

and you don't go down the snack aisle anymore.
Saving money while being healthy!!!!

56) **Importance to go to the dentist** I understand dentist visits cost anywhere from $70-200 a visit. But my father, who has no dental insurance, paid around $1000 for a root canal. The average root canal according to mykoolsmiles.com ranges from $957 to $1,184f for one tooth. It is important to keep up with regular cleanings to avoid costly dental and health bills in the future. Bad dental hygiene can lead to increase in other health problems like heart problems. Also, my dad did not go to the dentist most of his life and they are spending 1,000's of dollars on dental bills. Kids make sure you brush your teeth twice a day and floss. Also, my dentist said I'm prone to getting cavities. He wanted me to get another cleaning done each year that would not be covered by insurance $70-$200. I just went out and bought an electric toothbrush ($5) and that solved my problem.

57) **No select sports if you are in debt** Anymore, select sports are not select . Most select soccer organizations go 3 to 4 deep in each age bracket. The average is anywhere from $500 to $3000 a

year. To jump from the 3rd string team to first string team is not likely. When my daughter played for 2 years, the average cost was $1500 not including hotel and food. We would bring our own food and did not stay in hotels, we drove home. Now, select soccer does teach a great work ethic. My daughter was told if you're on time you're ten minutes late. It taught her to practice outside of team practices and taught her to set personal goals for herself. We paid $3000 to teach her to teach her to be hyper focused in school and Winterguard (She switched sports after she got 2nd team in soccer after being the leading scorer the year before). If we had to do it all over again, my daughter and I both agree, she would skip select sports altogether.

58) **Cut boys hair at home/girls hair grow long** I just started cutting my hair at home. It used to cost me $13 every 2 months or $78 a year. Now my wife and daughter get their haircut about 3 times a year. My hairdresser said anybody can trim up bangs. I trimmed up my daughter and brought her to the hairdresser 3 weeks later. My hairstylist advised me never to touch anybody's hair again. It was bad!! So, for boys/men that have a short haircut, a pair of

clippers for $15 at Wal-mart can save you $63 per person in the first year and $78 per person in the years after that. For girls/women, I would suggest keeping the hair longer. Have your haircut 3-4 times a year. Shop around for a reasonably priced hair stylist.

59) **Chromebooks** If you need a computer or your kid does, I would go to the library for free computer access. But in cases like now with coronavirus, I would buy a chromebook. It's a lot cheaper than a laptop or desktop. You can get one for $150 to $300. Also, the chromebook is almost virus proof. Chromebooks can use google docs for free. And they are very fast on the internet and great for streaming video..

60) **No paid internet- the library or netzero** The internet can be very costly per month. Spectrum costs $49 plus $9.99 for wi-fi. $60 x 12 equals $720 per year. For the first 12 years of our marriage we didn't pay for the internet (and we had no phones either). We needed to check emails and look up things from time to time at home so we used Netzero. You get 10 hours of internet time per month for free. There is a banner with ads. The speed is very slow

relative to what most people are used to (56K). During peak hours, it was extremely slow. We also went to the library to look up things. To this day, we do all of printing at the library. Printers are too expensive to maintain with the cost of ink.

61) **No new clothes** People can spend a lot of money on new clothes. For my daughter we got clothes from my sister (my mom would buy them off my sister to help her out and give the clothes to us to help us out), my mom, and bought used clothes up to the age of 7. We bought the cheapest shoes for my daughter because kids grow out of shoes so fast. We bought most of her shoes under $10. My wife and I still wear clothes from 20 years ago. We buy clothes the day after thanksgiving, using coupons,or we buy things for under $5 at the end of the season. Sometimes my mom wants to help out and I have no problem having her buy us an outfit every once a while. Also, Know your warranties. Most shoe companies have a warranty. Most are 1-2 years from manufacture date. If they fall apart or start having problems, contact the company and request a replacement. Most companies will have you send in the shoes at your cost to review the defect. If they

feel it's a defect, they will replace the shoe or give a voucher of the shoes value.

62) **No drinking** Drinking is an expensive habit also. Of course, drinking in a bar is more expensive than drinking at home. According to thebalanceeverday.com , the average american household spends $565 a year on alcohol or $5,650 on alcohol in 10 years. Yes, every once in a while I want to have a beer. We buy Busch light which you can buy for $18 for 30 cans- a one year supply for me. We try not to spend on things that you eat or drink because it all ends up in the same place.

63) **No downloading songs** You can download songs from most libraries. You can also check out cd's also. I never paid for downloading a song because I use the methods above. The average cost for streaming/downloading music like Amazon is $119 a rear. And streaming services cost from 5 to 15 dollars a month or $60 to $180 a year. I cringe that my daughter pays 60 dollars a year for Amazon music. She can listen to her songs for free on Youtube.

64) **No concerts** This statement refers to going out to bars, movies, or concerts. Concerts cost an

average $96 according to statista.com. If you go to 4 concerts per year for 2 people, it would cost $768 a year. That does not include parking, food/drinks,or T-shirts. I always look for free concerts in the summertime. Around holidays/festivals, there are a lot of cities that offer free concerts. Most artists at these events are from the 1980's, which I love the 80's. Early on in our marriage, I had to turn down a free concert because I was working a 2nd job at Miami Valley memory gardens as a telemarketer. I asked my manager for the night off and he said no. I needed the job. I couldn't make my house payment without this 2nd job. So, I missed out on the Outfield. Now I go to 5-10 concerts a year. My goal is to never miss a concert because I had to work a job. I love being front row center, but now I can go guilt free because I can afford it and I have met my goals!

65) **Watch sporting events at home, do not attend the event** I have a lot of friends that go to CIncinnati Bengals. Average ticket price is $99. Plus, you have parking, tailgating food and drink, and any food you drink/eat inside the stadium. If you do need afix of live sports, college games are less expensive

66) **College sports** - I said pro sports or minor league sporting events can be expensive. However, college sports can be more reasonable after you're debt free including your house and cars. After we paid off our house, I started to take my daughter to Bowling Green Events. You can get a Jr. Falcon Club for $30. This let's children 12 and under to attend all BGSU sporting events for only $30. BGSU flex plan 10 tickets for $90. For the first few years of going up, I paid a lot less than $9 a ticket (We started to go to every Hockey game and Football games). We would park in the student parking lot to get free parking. Past few years, we donated to the Falcon club and they offered free parking and free snacks at the hockey game for less than the price of season long parking at football and hockey. Megan got several chances to meet the coaches and ask what goals it takes to become a college athlete. She was kid coach of the game at the hockey game and asked Coach Chris Bergeron , hockey coach, what happened to her favorite player. The coach never sugar coated anything and told her he was kicked out due to grades. He dropped out and lost out on a great chance to be seen by the NHL. Having your

kids hear the importance of setting goals and the importance of hard work work is priceless.

67) **Discount Club's** I hate paying the price for them, but they are well worth it. For a $45 dollar Sam's club, you can split it with a friend. $22.5 a person. Tires are one of the best discounts you can buy at Sam's. I saved over $120 on tires compared to retail tire stores on a set of Michelin tires. We love breakfast sandwiches(Jimmy Dean delight). They are high in protein and a lot healthier than fast food. Also they are only $1 a piece. The socks are an awesome price there. Also, dishwashing soap is really discounted there. Aslo, I forgot how expensive cleaning supplies are (Clorox wipes) when you are trying to find them in a regular retailer.

68) **Thermostat** When we were first married, I kept the thermostat between 60-63. My wife and I were laying in bed one night after turning down the heat. She was cold and jokingly said she could probably see her breath. And we saw her breath. According to alpscomfortair.com , for every 1 degree you lower your thermostat you will save 3% on your heating bill. So if you go from 70 degrees to 60 degrees, you would save 30% on your heating bill. When we were

first married, we ran the air conditioner only at night. We would come into a warm trailer and air it out and then turn on the air conditioner. Then, I put styrofoam in the windows to insulate the trailer better. We ran the air conditioner all the time but turned it up when we were not there. And according to goldstarcooling.com, it is better to leave it at a constant temperature for air conditioners.

69) **Get to know the college admissions person for the college your child is applying for and ask for help finding scholarships to apply for** My daughter has thought about going to BGSU since she was kindergarten. (I have taken her to sporting events since she was 2). Whether she will go there or not she will go there who knows. But I can help my chances of getting her a full ride by talking to different admissions people and asking about different ways to find and apply to scholarships. In a few years, my daughter's job will be to apply to scholarships. It doesn't matter how big or small. It only matters that it covers her full college career. To make it easier to get scholarships, Megan, my daughter has studied very hard the past several years. She excels in Math because of all the different

ways I tried to trick her on her bed time. There was always a catch 22. If she could figure it out, she would get the extras time. Also we played a lot of board games when she was little. Turn off the TV and play games with your children. We are concentrating on BGSU right now because that is where she has expressed the most interest. We told her she had to pick an instate school that you could afford. Why pay 27,000 (47,000 for the same school if you are out of state) per year for in-state tuition when you can pay 24,000 a year for a cheaper school. Right now we know the person we need to talk to when Megan is ready to go to BGSU. I will make an appointment after she takes her SAT and ACT scores and see what scholarships are available both academic and other.

70) **Don't be afraid to put some sweat into something to save money-** In life, you have many choices. The more you pay other people to do something, the less money you will have. Don't be afraid of hard work. In the past we did landscaping over one summer that saved us 19,000. We knew someone that paid 20,000 for landscaping (they could afford it). So we wanted the same yard. We

planted everything ourselves and did all of the landscaping. We even delivered over 100 bags of mulch in 2 cars. After 2 years of doing that, the associate at the store, said we can deliver it to you for $70. That was worth it and still is to this day. A lot of sweat, but 20 years later we have the best looking yard in the neighborhood.   Also, this applies to other areas in my life, too. If I can save some money by being a little inconvenienced, then I will do it. We were on vacation in Spain. We stayed 30m minutes outside of town because the hotel was dirt cheap. (Side story,I bought the wrong rail pass and I was stopped by police. They took pity on us because we didn't have a pin to use our credit card to upgrade the rail pass). The only way to get to the cruise ship from the subway station was to walk about 2 miles to the cruise ship with our luggage over a tall bridge that a cruise ship could fit under). My wife was upset.

 Fast forward 3 year later, the same thing happened again. This time we had the cash but they wanted to charge us double the exchange rate because we had US dollars and I guess stupid written on our forehead. Again we walked over that bridge again.

 At Least this time I took a picture of Sally walking

behind me. Don't forget the past or you're doomed to repeat it. Have the correct currency on you in cash before the trip.

71) **Drive not fly to 1 star hotels**   Once we were debt free (paying off the mortgage), we started to take a few vacations/ cruises each year. One way we save money is by staying in 1 star hotels. We drive 16 hours to get on a cruise ship, so we would get a $60 hotel before we get on the cruise ship. We saved money by not flying to Miami ($200 to $300 a person= $600 to $900 as a family of 3). I have tried to drive on the day of a cruise and I'm too tired the first day on the cruise. We have stayed in hotels that advertise "We have color TV's or phones." The trip is 1,175 miles / 35 miles per gallon = 34 gallons x 2 (to get home)= 68 gallons x $2 per gallon= $136 + hotel cost $60 = $196. The savings driving even including the hotel is a $400-$700 savings!!!

72) **No expensive hotels**   When we went on vacations after we were out of debt including cars and our house, we stayed and still stay in cheap hotels. Hotels are places to sleep. We spend our vacation money to do activities, not a nice room to stay in. The one exception is Embassy suites in

Canada. We stay there when they send email specials for around $100-$120. You get happy hour, a free breakfast overlooking the falls- a $90 dollar value, and usually a putt putt/haunted house package worth $30 per person x 3 =$90. Plus, they give you a $25 dollar voucher to gamble. Just play there money and pull it out. I usually win $25-$50 from their money. Also, the room overlooks the falls which I stare at for hours. My wife hates to stay down by the falls for hours, so having a falls view room is priceless to her. Thanksgiving you can get the room at 50% percent off. We never go in season there because the rates double. If you can stay in a hotel away from the major attraction/ beach, you can save lots of money. I like using kayak.com to search several websites to find the best hotel price. Sally is happy if she sees just more than one star next to the hotel we book!

73) **No debt** If you're in debt, see Dave Ramsey. He has the best plan to get out of debt. I have lived my whole life avoiding debt at all cost. We went into debt for 1 car and a house that we paid off in 10 years. If you stay out of debt, there is no interest you are giving to the banks and credit card companies.

You use that money to invest and to achieve your goals. Average U.S. households pay $1,162 in credit interest per year (nerdwallet.com) and pay $4,333 in mortgage interest (based on a 30 year loan with 7% interest). That is $5,495 for the average American that has a house and credit card payment. That does not include car debt. What could you do with $5,495 dollars a year. You have money to invest in Roth IRA's, vacations, and a chance to get a head/ breathe!!!!

74) **Go to friends houses and watch movies/hangout/ game night** Some of my favorite times are just sitting around and having dinner or a beer with family or friends. Before my in-laws passed away, we would watch a Nascar Race/ take a nap and then talk around the table for a few hours. These days families don't spend undistracted time with each other. They look at their phones. Now, we met with my mom and dad sometimes just for a drink somewhere to socialize. I told my daughter, we'll have her family over for pizza once a week and watch the Bengals. The past several years I go and see my best friend in his band. I don't drink. I pay the

cover if there is a cover and just enjoy friends and music.

75) **"Everything counts in large amounts"** This is one of my favorite Depeche Mode songs. I live my life by this motto. You watch the everyday small spendings because the smalls everyday coffee's or eating out will cost you more than some of your bigger purchases. You get all your small spending under control by getting on a budget. We set our grocery budget at $20, eating out $0, cell phone $0, $0 cable bill, $0 movies/dvd's, $0 smoking, $0 drinking, $0 on the internet, ect. How much money would you save if you set your budget to zero for all those things I listed above? How much money could you put towards your retirement or your kids 529 plans? How many goals could you accomplish?

76) **No gambling/lottery** " Everything counts" If your goal was life or death, you would have a very detailed budget where every cent is accounted for. Friends say it's only $2 a week or $104 a year. If you gamble $50 a week at the casino, you would spend $2600 in one year. I belonged to a club where I would watch football games. They had the best drinks for $2.25. At this private club, they had a $5

raffle. Most people were just getting by. However they would spend $260 a year gambling on a raffle. At the same club, they had football pools where it would cost $50-$100 a square. They constantly had different ways to gamble/throw your life away. This is insane!!! I went to Vegas 9 times and spent $5 dollars in gambling for all the trips. Don't waste your money: 1 in 13,983,816 win the lottery (wikipedia) and the odds of getting hit by lightning is 1 to 700,000 (nationalgeographic.com). You have a better chance of getting hit by lightning twice than you have at winning the lottery.

77) **Contribute to your work's retirement up to the match** One of the easiest ways to invest is using your work 401k or pension program. They usually match your contribution dollar for dollar up to a certain dollar amount. Each company decides how much they match. Invest up to the match. Then, I would open a Roth IRA. Roth IRA's are retirement accounts where you use post taxed money (money in your bank account) to invest in retirement. It grows tax free. You can take out the original investment anytime without penalties/taxes. When you become 59 ½, you can withdraw the full amount without owing

taxes. After you invest your full amount in your Roth ($6000 per year), put any extra money you have into mutual funds like an index 500 (13% in the past 10years)

78) **Don't look at your stock portfolio except a few times a year** Mutual funds will go up and down depending on economic growth ,interest rates, stability in society, confidence and expectations, and markets reacting to certain events, and a company's earnings. In a given week, a mutual fund can go up and down several times throughout the week. What you have to look at is how the stock performs over many years like 10-20. This past year I was down 20% at one time. Every month I would check in on it. Surprise surprise just yesterday, the markets were in the red for the year 2020. Think of it like monopoly money. You want to win the game, but you can't obsess over it on a daily basis. I like the Index 500 because it has a long track record of doing well (13% over the past 10 years).

79) **Be wary of any recurring monthly bill**   I hate recurring monthly bills. If you can trim the bill by $5 a month, That's a $60 saving for the year. I'm always calling the companies every few months to see if

there is a cheaper plan for electricity, heating, ADT, ect. Most of them you can save $5-$20 a month which is $110-$240 a year. I'm constantly looking at the big goal and trying to shave off as much waste as possible.

80) **Go to church**   I feel if you are good to other people and treat other people right, you will be rewarded by having more opportunities available to you. Going to church teaches you/ reminds of good moral virtues that we should live by. And sometimes they have a free breakfast (donuts).

81) **Hang around successful people**   I have always been drawn to successful people. I married somebody that has skills I don't have. I work with successful people. My best friend is one of the best cover band singers out there. You become like the people you hang out. I love to hang out with my parents because they have always been wise with budgeting. However I had to explain my comments that my daughter said to my parents after spending the night with them. Megan told my parents that their car was not a wise decision to own because it was too expensive. We had to explain to her that my parents did make a wise decision but for us because

we made so much less than my parents it would be a bad decision. In fact, my dad bought a used car which saved several thousands dollars by not taking the depreciation of a new car. We explained to her it is affordable to them and he got a great deal on it. I ,also, had to smooth things over with my parents- was giving me a hard time jokingly the first time she told me this.

82) **Take public transportation when on vacation**

After we were out of debt including our house and cars, we started to travel. I will drive anywhere on the east coast, but we have to fly to Europe and the West coast. We have taken subways, trains, buses, and as a last resort an Uber, If we are sight seeing, we will get a cheap rental car. I remember one time, we got a steal of a deal on a rental car, but it was a clown car. It had no trunk and a very small back seat. We barely got the three of us in the car with our suitcases. In Spain we took the train to zone 3 because hotels in the city were very expensive. I will even drive 8 hours to an amusement park to stay 6 hours and drive home 8 hours to avoid the hotel fee. Thank God for Mountain Dew.

83) Find free entertainment- walks, parks, free movies, and the library   Some of the best things in life are free. Going for nature walks around your neighborhood or state parks are awesome ways to destress and for free. I've noticed a lot of wealthier people are goal oriented towards their finances and their fitness. These people have a drive to stay fit both economically and physically.   76% of people that are rich exercise for at least 30 minutes daily, according to Tom Corley, author of "Change Your Habits, Change Your Life." After you exercise for free by running outside, you can pick up a free movie or book at the library. Want a particular movie or book, you can request it. This saves time!

84) Stay healthy   When you stay healthy you have less medical expenses and you have less missed days at work. If you exercise, get sleep, eat right, watch your weight, don't smoke, don't drink, and watch your stress levels, you can take control of your health and life. You can save money on medication that you won't have to take because your health is in good condition. If you stay healthy, you're able to enjoy more activities in life. When you stay healthy, you are able to live longer to enjoy your wealth.

85) No private school/ yes to daycare   I went to a private school for elementary and highschool. I feel it's more about positive peer pressure your child has from their friends. If they hand around studious people, then your child is more likely to care about their studies. If they hang around friends that do drugs, they have a greater chance of doing drugs. Raising a child is the biggest pet peeve of mine. Parents put effort into their kids until school age and then they seem to give up. Our daughter is at the top of her school; scored perfect on the state test twice in Math and scored advanced always; and skipped two grades in Math. So, I feel my wife and I can speak on this subject. My daughter did not watch TV for the first 2 years of her life (no Barney or Sesame Street). We turned off the TV when she was awake. We played with her and did activities with her. We had her in a daycare with a person out of their home that did daycare for several other teacher's kids. She has played with kids every day since she was 3 months old. She attended preschool. When she went to kindergarten it was only a ½ day. We had her in a daycare kinder kindergarten for the other half. We read to her. But even doing all that she started to fall behind in Reading In 2nd grade. She didn't know her site words. I looked at her and said if you can learn of your 2nd grade site words, I'll buy you any toy at Toys R us. She learned all of her sight words in 2 weeks; jumped up 2 Reading levels in that time; and I bought her a toy that cost me $5 dollars. The best $5 I've ever spent. We liked to get bonuses at work and I don't mind rewarding Megan every once in a while for her hard work. For math we played Board game after board game. One time I said she could stay up until I won at Rummy Cubes. She usually never won, but that night she was on a hot streak and finally I said it's 11:30 time to go to bed. I'll give you 2 weekend night's to stay up. In the car, I always quizzed her on her Math facts. I would always try to trick her out of her bed time and if she could figure out the trick, she could stay up (different time zones, daylight savings, ect.). Since she was 4, we have been traveling all summer. Megan has never sat in front of the TV all summer. We went to kids museums, amusement parks, skiing, and traveled (a lot of trips would have 16 hour car rides to spend plenty of family time). I would recommend: no TV the first 2 years of a child's life, spend lots of time playing games with them, daycare (the 2nd income is awesome along with socialization skills for your child/ having to listen to adults other than a family member); and do lots of activities with them.

86) **Make homemade food** It's cheaper to make homemade food; iit tastes better,and it is healthier for you. People worry about catching the flu and the coronavirus. One of the best ways as a teacher I found to stay healthy is to get plenty of sleep.   I'm constantly exposed to germs and viruses. I use lemon juice instead of cough syrup. Also, I eat plenty of blueberries in blueberry muffins. Of course, they are expensive. Once a year I buy them when they go on sale in the first 2 week of June. I used to get a quart for 99 cents, but nowI can only get them for $1.49-$2.

Here are my families 2 favorite recipe pumpkin bread (we grow our on pumpkins) and blueberry muffins:

Blueberry muffins: 2 cups of flour, 3 teaspoon of baking powder, ½ Teaspoon of salt, ½ cup of sugar, 1 egg, 1 cup of milk, 6 tablespoons of butter, and 2 cups of blueberries. Mix all ingredients into a bowl. After mixing, add the blueberries. Grease muffin pans and bake at 400 degrees for 15 to 20 minutes. Sprinkle sugar on after 10 minutes of baking. Pumpkin Bread: sift 1 ⅔ c of flour, 1 ½ cof sugar, 1 teaspoon of baking soda, ½ teaspoon cinnamon, ½ teaspoon of nutmeg, ¼ teaspoon of salt. Mix ingredients with ½ cup copped ?, 2 egg beaten, ½ c of oil,⅓ c of water and 1 c of pumpkin. Ix til blended. Put in a muffin pan at 350 for 20-25 minutes.

87) **Check To see if there is a discount if you pay in full** We received a 10% discount on my daughters braces just because we asked about discounts. They assumed we were going to finance them When I said I'll pay in full, they offered us a 10% discount. Also, I always ask if there is a union discount or a teacher discount. They usually laugh but then they say sometimes, :``We have this promotion……." Score!!!!!!!!!

88) **Take public transportation during vacations** During our vacations, we always take buses and subways even with our luggage. Once you're out of debt, vacations can be a blessing. Just because I'm on vacation, I don't stop doing Math. If I can find plan B to get me to my destination, I'll do it. In New York, Vancoover, Paris and Barcelona we always take

subways and buses. It might take longer and is a pain in the butt to haul your luggage on public transportation, but it is so much cheaper than taking a taxi.

89) **Eggs, bread, milk** When we were saving for a big goal like a new house (my wife wanted out of the trailer so bad) and in vitro. We cut our grocery budget to under $20 a week. We cut every bill we had because these two goals were so important to us that we were willing to sacrifice everything. If you really wanted to retire early, I would sacrifice today for the goal tomorrow. That is wacky. Most people borrow tomorrow's future to do something today by using credit cards and loans. We lived in one of the worst trailers in the trailer park because lot rent was $125 and we could reach our goals faster by sacrificing today for our goals tomorrow. I was talking to a friend on PS4 that was having trouble replacing a cracked disc that cost $15 dollars to replace. He spends all his money even though he makes great money as a heating and air guy. People need to set goals and get on a budget.

90) **Cheap rent (trailer)** My wife and I knew our goal was to own a house before we were married.

We did not have enough money for the down payment, so we wanted our rent as cheap as possible. It just so happened my sister was selling her trailer she lived in after college for a few years to save up for a house. My mother gave her $5,000 dollars for her down payment and gave us $5,000 to pay my sister for the trailer. My mom wanted me out of the house when I graduated college. I made too much noise at night time. My sister's house was 11 months delayed and I got to stay at my parents' place rent free!! I did pass my mom on the way to bed when she was getting up several times. The lot rent was $125 x 12 months= $1,500 a month or $3,000 for 2 years. Rent was going for $350-$400 at apartments I looked at back then ($375 x 12= $4,500x2 years =$9,000. $9,000-$3,000= a $6,000 savings we had by staying in the worst trailer in the trailer park and not getting a nice apartment like all of our friends had. That $6,000 got us into a nicer home than any of our friends. Don't try to keep up with Jones, be the Jones!!!

91) **Return the gift if you don't like it or re gift it to someone else**

When my daughter was born, we exchanged every gift we did not want. Now there were some clothes and gifts we did not find the store that the person bought it from. No worries. After 13 years, we just gave away our last baby item we had to a babyshower. We haven't spent any money on baby showers for 13 years. We average 4 baby showers a year at $20 a gift = $80 a year x 13 years= $1040. That is about what it cost us to go to disney 10 years ago. A free Disney trip with the family because we gave away something we would never use= priceless family memories.

92) **No lessons** When my daughter was 4 or 5, we signed her up for dance lessons. Dance lessons cost about $60 to $150 a month or $720 to $1,800 a year. This does not include all the costumes, shoes, ect. If you don't own your home, you have credit card debt, or you have a car loan, then you can't afford to have your kids in lessons. Personally I couldn't tell the difference from my daughter, who was in it for 1 month, compared to kids that were in 3 to 4 years. I understand you want your kids to participate in school activities. Lots of schools will loan out there instruments and will work with your child during

school. Swim clubs are even worse. The average swim club in my area cost around $3,000 by the time you pay your annual registration, annual USA-Swimming Membership/Insurance: Registration is $163, annual swim membership $77, and Monthly Training: $240= $3,128 a year. You shouldn't be spending $3,000 on a swim team if you still have student loans or any other debt. According to the Washington Post, 70% of all kids quit organized sports by the age of 13.

93) **Use energy saving light bulbs** I always make sure I turn off the lights when I leave the room. But you get more bang for your buck to replace old light bulbs with cfl bulbs/ led bulbs. In one year, you can save 100's of dollars according to blog.arcadia.com. If you have a 100w incandescent bulb at 15 cents per KWH and use 876 KWH of energy, it would cost you $131.40. A 25w cfl (same brightness) uses 216 KWP would cost you $32.40. A LED bulb 16w (same brightness) would use only 140 KWH and cost you only $21 a month. Yes, the LED bulbs cost more at the store, but you will make it up in electricity savings. It's good for the environment and your pocket book. Our house already had a lot of CFL bulbs, but we

switched the remaining of the bulbs with more efficient ones. I just got 4 led bulbs on sale for $0.99. It pays to look for deals!

94) **Sleep in airports** I asked my daughter what was one worst way I try to save money- sleeping in airports. We have had several overnight layovers because the flights become cheaper if you're willing to take layovers and more connecting flights. We always buy the cheapest airfare and end up in the last row of the plane where the seats don't recline. However, we had a 10 hour layover in Paris that gave us the opportunity to see/go up to the top of the Eiffel tower in Paris. We were living on snacks we brought with us and we took the subway from the airport to the Eiffel tower. We had an awesome time in Paris but my daughter still remembers having to sleep in the Paris Airport. I always ask her how many people get the chance to go up in the Eiffel Tower. Our family goal was to see the Eiffel tower, not to stay in a hotel room in Paris.

95) **Don't hold grudges/ Don't waste time** Life is too short. You could die tomorrow. If you waste time on a grudge that is precious time away from you enjoying life and completing your goals. Most of the

time, the other person that offended you has moved on and has forgotten about the situation. Too much time in a person is spent worrying about what happened and or what is going to happen. If you just live life and try to meet your goals, you will have more time to be successful. My wife knows I don't say angry at anyone- it's not worth my time. After the 6 brain surgeries, I learned anger is such a time waster. If we have a disagreement, let's talk out a solution. And yes sometimes my wife and I agree to disagree.

96) **No makeup** I love my wife's natural beauty. My wife and I are not fans of makeup. Today she was applying her expensive lip bomb. It was a Hello Kitty lip bomb that my daughter Megan had 10 years ago. We all got a laugh at it. The average woman spends $3756 per year or $225,360 over her lifetime (byrdie.com). You could buy a house if you use no makeup. That is insane. What goal is more important to you- do you want to hide your true look/ natural beauty or a house. This stat shocked me.

97) **No subscriptions to PS4, Netflix, Disneyplus, ect** People usually tell me it's a great value or it's only a few dollars a month to have one of these

subscriptions. PS4 is $42 a year times 10 years and that's $420. Netflix is $9 to $16. Let's say you pick the cheaper one. 9 x 12= $98. Over 10 years, you have spent almost $1000 dollars on Netflix!! Disney plus is only $70 a year or $700 dollars per 10 years. By cutting these constant bills out of your life, you will have more money to invest and meet your goals. One of my goals is to retire when I want to retire. I can give up my goal of binge watching Tiger King to achieve my goal of retiring in my 50's

98) **Make a list of every expense and have your spouse approve and disapprove the expense** If you truly are serious about becoming a millionaire or achieving a big goal, you need to review all your expenses with your spouse. I can't have the freedom to go out and get a cup of coffee even at ...... (5 days a week x 52 weeks= 260 days x $2.15, average price of coffee according to cartacoffee.com, = $560 x 2 people =$1120). No wonder why Americans are broke. They buy too many drinks out at stores. We talk over all purchases. We have a set list of approved groceries and household items that when they are low, one of us will go out and get it. We know what brand is the best value and what store to

get it at. There is only one time that we have ever strayed away from this. I bought a Basketball machine game for 75% off and my wife bought a pair of snow boots. They both arrived in the mail about a day apart from each other. I said you keep yours and I'll keep mine. I would never go to the store and pick up a 12 pack of donuts and bring them home without discussing it with Sally. We still have common goals and you can't nickel and dime the budget to achieve all your goals. We set big goals so we don't mind sacrificing the small things. We can afford pinball machines because we don't buy coffee out for 6 years. I dream big so the little stuff doesn't matter to me. I have no problem spending $30,000 on vacations for a summer or $6000 dollars on a pinball machine, but I do have a problem with buying a value meal out when we could eat for a lot cheaper at home.

99) **Be generous** In life, people like being around generous people. People are drawn towards generous people. My wife and I are very stringent with the budget, but we find ways to be generous. I have taken people to concerts, amusement parks, and events that they couldn't afford to go to. I even

offered to pay for my best friend to go on a cruise at my expense. We still donate to the church, but I like donating directly like leaving a $50 dollar tip for dinner on a cruise ship. The bigger organizations are great to donate to, but they have overhead and other expenses. I like to donate directly to people.

100) **Keep it simple and stay focused on your goal** You need to remember to eliminate all costs from your budget that are not necessary. You need to get a 2nd job or switch your career to increase your income. Remember the No's (no cable, no cell phones, no restaurants, no non-essential purchases, no vacations, no new clothes and no debt). Remember the must haves (a budget, income, investing, a plan to increase income while lowering expenses, and GOALS!!!!!!!!!!!). What are your dreams/goals in life? Set your goals and the steps to achieve them.

101) **No happy meals**
The first sale of this e-book, I promised my daughter I would buy her first chicken nugget happy meal. One time, a friend said I feel sorry for Megan because I have never bought her a happy meal. I responded by saying I feel sorry for you kid because your kid has

never been to Alaska, Hawaii, Italy, Spain, Caribbean, Mexico and Paris (France). I never bought a happy meal for my daughter, but she has been to the top of the Eiffel Tower. Goals- is your goal for your family to eat happy meals or travel the world! You decide your goals! Set your dreams/ goals today so you can achieve them in the future.